AF177607

Mathijs van Alstein

Die Zukunftskraft des Unvollendeten

The Promise of the Unfinished

Mathijs van Alstein

Die Zukunftskraft des Unvollendeten
The Promise of the Unfinished

Ausgabe in deutscher und englischer Sprache

Urachhaus

LOGOS-edition, Band 1
November 2022

ISBN 978-3-8251-5364-9

Erschienen 2022 im Verlag Urachhaus
www.urachhaus.com

 Entdecken Sie weitere Bücher aus dem Verlags-
bereich Religiöse Erneuerung und Kulturgeschicht
urachhaus.de/religion

Liebe Leserinnen und Leser,

mit dem vorliegenden Beitrag von Mathijs van Alstein erreicht Sie der erste Band der neuen LOGOS-edition im Verlag Urachhaus. Diese neue Reihe geht auf die internationale Tagung der Christengemeinschaft zum Beginn ihres zweiten Jahrhunderts im Oktober 2022 in Dortmund zurück.

Die Begeisterung der über 2.500 Teilnehmer an verschiedenen inhaltlichen Beiträgen führte zu der Idee, einige der dort gehaltenen Vorträge zu verschriftlichen und einem größeren Kreis von Leserinnen und Lesern zugänglich zu machen.

Während der Vorbereitung der neuen Edition kam scherzhaft – aber durchaus treffend – die Wendung »Veröffentlichung aus dem Zukunftsarchiv der Christengemeinschaft« ins Spiel. Bereits während der Tagung, aber auch beim späteren Sichten der Vortragsabschriften hatten wir immer wieder den Eindruck, dass die »lehrende Seele« der Christengemeinschaft, von der Rudolf Steiner 1922 sprach, hier durch den Mund der vielen Redner auf vielfältige Art und Weise aus der Zukunft heraus wieder spricht.

Unser großer Dank gilt Michael Stehle und dem Verlag Urachhaus, die unsere Idee freudig aufnahmen und die zeitnahe Herausgabe der LOGOS-edition ermöglichten. Danken möchten wir auch Isabel Becker und Ulrich Meier für die Übernahme der redaktionellen Arbeit. Nicht zuletzt gilt unser Dank jedoch den Vortragsrednern für die Bearbeitung und Durchsicht der Manuskripte. So können ab November 2022 etwa im monatlichen Rhythmus weitere Ausgaben folgen und als Inspirationsquelle anregend für das zweite Jahrhundert der Christengemeinschaft weiterwirken.

Die Herausgeber
Martin Merckens – Jarosław J. J. Rolka
Stuttgart und Bochum, 11. November 2022

Dear Readers,

with the present contribution by Mathijs van Alstein, you have received the first volume of the new LOGOS-edition published by Urachhaus. This new series of small books stems from the international conference of the Christian Community beginning its second century, which took place in October 2022 in Dortmund, Germany.

It was the warm interest and enthusiasm of the more than 2,500 participants for various contents that led us to the idea of putting some of the lectures given at the conference on paper and making them accessible to a wider circle of readers.

In preparing the new edition, the phrase »Publications from the Future Archive of the Christian Community« came into play, jokingly but quite appropriately. Already during the conference, but also as we reviewed the lecture transcripts, we repeatedly had the impression that the »teaching soul« of the Christian Community, of which Rudolf Steiner spoke in 1922, is speaking again through the voices and hearts of the many speakers in many different ways coming from the future.

Our great thanks go to Michael Stehle and the publishing house Urachhaus, who joyfully accepted our idea and made the rapid publication of the LOGOS-edition possible. We would also like to thank Isabel Becker and Ulrich Meier for taking on the editorial work. Last but not least, we would like to thank the speakers for their work in editing and reviewing the manuscripts. This way, from November 2022 onwards, further volumes will follow at about monthly intervals and continue to act as a source of inspiration for the second century of the Christian Community.

The editors
Martin Merckens – Jarosław J. J. Rolka
Stuttgart and Bochum, 11.11.2022

Mathijs van Alstein

Die Zukunftskraft des Unvollendeten

Liebe Freunde!

In diesem Jahr 2022 ist es genau hundert Jahre her, dass 1922 das gesprochene Wort völlig neue Wirkungsmöglichkeiten bekam. Denn in diesem Jahr, genauer gesagt im Oktober 1922, wurde in London die BBC gegründet. Als ich noch ein Kind war in den Achtzigerjahren, habe ich mir gerne am Abend im Radio lokale Programme angehört, und da wurde manchmal gesagt: »Liebe Leute, wir sind wieder im Äther!« Rückblickend kann es gewiss kein Zufall gewesen sein, dass die BBC und Die Christengemeinschaft in genau dem gleichen Jahr gegründet wurden, mehr oder weniger in den gleichen Wochen sogar. Wir können in der Tat heute sagen: Vor hundert Jahren hat sich die Ätherwelt so geöffnet, dass Moderatoren in ein Mikrofon sprechen konnten und dadurch Hunderttausende, ja Millionen Haushalte erreichten; zur gleichen Zeit hat sich die Ätherwelt so geöffnet, dass in ihr das neue kultische Wort ertönen konnte. Beide Ereignisse, das technische und das kultische, scheinen zusammen zu gehören. In den hundert Jahren, auf die wir heute zurückblicken, haben die Medien eine rasante Entwicklung durchgemacht. In den Konsequenzen dieser Entwicklung stehen wir alle drinnen, und niemand wird noch behaupten, dass diese Folgen erfreulich sind. In den Achtzigerjahren des 19. Jahrhunderts hat ein deutscher Philosoph ein wunderbares Wort geprägt. Dieser Philosoph hieß Friedrich Nietzsche, und er hat 1882 geschrieben: »Noch ein Jahrhundert Zeitungen – und alle Worte stinken.«[1] In der Zeit, in der wir heute stehen, müssen wir sagen, dass da schon etwas dran gewesen ist. Wir haben nicht nur im finanziellen Bereich Inflationen gehabt – heute braucht man siebzehn Dollar, wo 1922 ein Dollar gereicht hat –, auch das Wort ist allmählich weniger wert geworden. Vielleicht stinken heute nicht alle Worte; immerhin ist klar, wie selten ein rein gesprochenes oder geschriebenes Wort geworden ist. In diese Welt, in der die Medien ihre unglaubliche Entwicklung durchgemacht haben, ist die Christengemeinschaft mit ihrem kultischen Wort hineingestellt. Seit hundert Jahren kommen wir regelmäßig zusammen, jeder in dem ihm geeigneten Rhythmus, um das gesprochene Wort im Weltenäther völlig untechnologisch hören zu können.

---

[1] Fr. Nietzsche, *Nachgelassene Fragmente*. Sommer-Herbst 1882.

Wie ist es beschaffen mit diesem kultischen Wort? Das Wort der Menschenweihehandlung, das uns allen sehr lieb ist, wird gesprochen aus einem Wesen heraus. Dieses Wesen nennt sich das Weltenwort, der Logos. Aus dem großen Sprechen des Weltenalls ertönt auf den Lippen des zelebrierenden Priesters ein Destillat dieses waltenden Weltenwortes. Damit wird die Menschenweihehandlung zu einem Wesen innerhalb eines Wesens, denn nicht nur der Logos ist wesenhaft, auch die Menschenweihehandlung ist eine eigenständige Wesenheit.

Haben wir diese Wesenheit als solche schon erkannt? Sind wir ihr schon vollbewusst begegnet? Gelingen wird diese Erkenntnisbegegnung auf jeden Fall nur, wenn wir in Betracht ziehen, dass die Weihehandlung älter ist als 1922, also schon da war, lange bevor die Christengemeinschaft gegründet wurde. Wie sollen wir das verstehen? Man kann sagen, dass die Menschenweihehandlung eine übersinnliche Säule ist, die sich durch die Jahrhunderte hindurch bewegt. Es ist sogar nicht falsch zu behaupten, dass diese Säule älter ist als die Tat Christi, die sie täglich feiert. Denn die Weihehandlung hat es gegeben, seit es Menschen gibt, die von ihren Göttern gnadenvoll begleitet werden, das heißt: seit den Uranfängen der Menschheit. Dieser Pfeiler der Menschenweihehandlung, der sich nicht nur Jahrhunderte, sondern schon Jahrtausende stützend betätigt, ist ein Wesen, das sich in seinen Metamorphosen bewusst und selbstbewusst ist. Wem gehört dieses Bewusstsein? Es gehört den Göttern selbst. Eine bestimmte Hierarchie dieser erhabenen Wesenheiten, die sehr wichtig ist, um der Menschenweihehandlung als selbstbewusstes Wesen gerecht zu werden, sind die Geister der Form, die *Exousiai*, zu denen im Alten Testament auch die Elohim gehören. Wer sind diese Geister der Form? Was verwalten sie? Das griechische Wort für Form ist *eîdos,* das heißt Idee. Sowohl bei Plato als bei Aristoteles sind die Ideen Wesenheiten, die wichtiger sind als die materielle Welt, wichtiger und wirklicher. Bei Plato sind sie mehr außerhalb unserer Welt zu finden, bei Aristoteles mehr in dieser Welt, aber beide Denker waren sich darin einig, dass die Ideen, die wohlgemerkt nicht etwas vom Menschen Hervorgebrachtes sind, den Grund der Welt bilden. Erst wenn wir ernst nehmen, dass die Weihehandlung ein selbstbewusstes Wesen ist, eine Idee, eine Form, die sich mehr unsichtbar als sichtbar durch die Jahrhunderte hindurchbewegt, können wir verstehen, wieso es in ihr heißen kann, dass in uns Christi Leidenstod denkt, dass in uns seine Offenbarung und seine Auferstehung denken. Denn in der Weihehandlung denken und fühlen nicht nur *wir*, sondern *werden* wir auch *gedacht und gefühlt* von geistigen Wesen! Diese Geister der Form, die die Ideen im Kosmos verwalten, dabei uns Menschen in ihre Gedanken und Gefühle aufnehmend, haben nun über sich eine andere Hierarchie. Diese Hierarchie nennt sich die *Dynameis*, die Geister der Bewegung. Auch sie ist für uns sehr bedeutend. Die Christengemeinschaft ist ja nicht nur eine Formangelegenheit, was in dem Kultus mit Händen zu greifen ist, sie ist auch – und sogar zutiefst – eine Bewegung. Wir nennen uns wahrlich nicht umsonst eine »Bewegung für religiöse Erneuerung«. Wenn wir die Christengemeinschaft richtig verstehen wollen, dann müssen wir also sagen: Sie ist Form innerhalb von Bewegung, genau wie die Geister der Form sich innerhalb von Geistern der Bewegung betätigen. Die Bewegung umhüllt die Form. So ist es bei den Hierarchien da oben, und so soll es auch sein bei uns hier unten. Die Christengemeinschaft will Form in Bewegung sein.

Es ist eine sehr bemerkenswerte Sache, dass Rudolf Steiner wenige Stunden, nachdem die Christengemeinschaft gegründet wurde, in dem Moment, wo all diese jungen Männer und Frauen wieder aus Dornach fortgegangen waren, einen Vortrag hielt, in dem er noch einmal über Kultus und kultische Handlungen sprach, jetzt nicht mehr zu werdenden Priestern, selbstverständlich, sondern zu Anthroposophen, die an der Gründung der Christengemeinschaft nicht teilgenommen hatten und mit der religiösen Erneuerung deswegen nicht verbunden waren. Der letzte Vortrag bei der Gründung wurde gehalten am 22. September 1922. Am 24. September 1922, also nicht mehr als 48 Stunden, nachdem das uralte Wesen der Menschenweihehandlung ein neues Gewand bekommen hatte, war Rudolf Steiner in der Lage, scheinbar unbeeindruckt von dem Großen, das sich gerade ereignet hatte, völlig nüchtern zu reden über die Gefahren, die mit kultischen Formen verbunden sind. Dieser Vortrag steht nicht in den Zyklen über die Christengemeinschaft, und man kann ihn deshalb leicht übersehen. Was da gesagt wurde, ist aber sehr wichtig, und ich meine, wir sollen dessen Inhalt als einen integralen Bestandteil unserer Gründungsgeschichte aufnehmen. Rudolf Steiner spricht in diesem Vortrag über die ägyptischen Mysterien und wie in ihnen mit der Mumie gewirkt wurde.[2] Weil die gesamte Moderne eine Metamorphose oder eine Art Wiederholung der ägyptischen Kultur darstellt, soll es uns nicht wundern, dass auch die Mumie, beziehungsweise ihre Atrophie, metamorphosiert zurückkehrt in der Moderne. Und da sagt Rudolf Steiner – ich möchte wiederholen, innerhalb von achtundvierzig Stunden, nachdem die Chris-

---

2 Rudolf Steiner, GA 216: *Die Grundimpulse des weltgeschichtlichen Werdens der Menschheit*, 5. Vortrag.

tengemeinschaft gegründet wurde: Die metamorpho-
sierte Mumie ist der Kultus! Er spricht da freilich über
verkommene katholische und Freimaurer-Rituale. Immerhin ist es sehr schwer, diese Aussage nicht auch als
eine Warnung hinzunehmen. Denn wieso musste gerade, nachdem die Menschenweihehandlung neu geboren
war, wieso musste wenige Stunden, nachdem sie sich re-
inkarniert hatte, über ihren möglichen Tod gesprochen
werden? Auch ein Kultus kann erstarren und zum toten
Objekt werden, in dem allerlei Geister und Gespens-
ter ihr Unwesen treiben. Diese Möglichkeit hat Rudolf
Steiner unmittelbar nach der Gründung der Christengemeinschaft offensichtlich sehr beschäftigt. Da ist natür-
lich die logische Frage: Wie stirbt denn ein Kultus? Der
Kultus stirbt, so können wir sagen, wenn seine Formen
stärker werden als das Leben, das sie zum Ausdruck
bringen sollen, das heißt, wenn er nicht länger in der
Lage ist, Form in Bewegung zu sein, sondern stattdes-
sen ausblutet, indem er irgendwelche Beweglichkeit innerhalb von vorgegebenen Formen wird.

Liebe Freunde, damit ist meiner Meinung nach nicht
etwas Kleines ausgesagt! Wir können die Warnung Rudolf Steiners, denn so verstehe ich den Vortrag von 24.
September, auch so hinnehmen, dass es sich hundert
Jahre nach der Gründung der Christengemeinschaft
nie darum handeln kann, dass unsere Bewegung für

religiöse Erneuerung zu einer Art ätherischem Bunker wird, in dem die Gläubigen zusammenkuscheln, um sich zu wehren gegen eine böse Welt, die sie außerdem am liebsten so fern wie möglich halten. Denn wenn wir derart Bewegung innerhalb von Form werden, wenn wir also Formen haben, die wir zwar lieben, aber so lieben, dass wir erst in ihnen, in diesen Formen, innerlich beweglich werden, dann tun wir dem Kultus ein Unrecht an. Dann haben wir die Form über die Bewegung gestellt. Gerade das ist bei den Hierarchien nicht der Fall, und ich meine, wir wären schlecht beraten, die Beziehungen zwischen Form und Bewegung unten anders zu gestalten als oben.

Wie schaffen wir es denn, Form in Bewegung zu sein, statt Bewegung in Form? Das Bild, das mir hier vor Augen schwebt, ist schlicht, muss ich gestehen, aber trotzdem, so scheint es mir, nicht unrichtig. Es soll sich darum handeln, dass wir eine Beweglichkeit finden, wobei wir in diese Formen des Kultus hereinkommen, uns da auch wohl fühlen, ganz gewiss, aber dies nicht, ohne ständig in der Lage zu bleiben, aus diesen Formen *wieder herauszukommen*, wie die Bienen, die in einen Bienenkorb hineingehen und da ihr Geschäft treiben, um dann auch wieder herauszugehen, in die weite Welt hinein. Wenn wir das tun, wenn wir unsere Religiosität so gestalten, dass wir uns sowohl innerhalb als auch außerhalb der kultischen Formen betätigen, dann steht die Form im Dienste des Lebens und nicht umgekehrt. Denn genau so soll es sein. Das Neue Testament nennt die Gemeinde die *ekklesia*. Ekklesia stammt von ek-ka-lein, was »herausrufen« bedeutet. Das heißt, dass wir als Gemeinde die Herausgerufenen sind, nicht die Hereingerufenen! Wir sollen uns deswegen nicht gegen eine böse Welt wehren, indem wir in der Kirche Schutz suchen, sondern wir sollen die bunte Vielfalt der ganzen Wirklichkeit integrieren, uns zutiefst mit ihr verbinden. Nur so kann die fortwährende Neugründung der Christengemeinschaft wahrhaft realisiert werden.

Ein Kollege von mir, Tom Tritschel, hat diesbezüglich auf einer Synode in Berlin etwas gesagt, was mich sehr begeistert hat, und er wird es mir bestimmt nicht übelnehmen, dass ich ihn hier heute zitiere. Christus sagt, dass er alles neu macht.[3] Das aber, sagte Tom, sollen wir als eine Totalaussage auffassen. Wenn er *alles* neu macht, macht er auch *sich selbst* neu. Darüber hatte ich noch nie nachgedacht, aber der Gedanke berührte mich unmittelbar. *Alles* bedeutet eben *alles*, oder nicht? Wie aber macht Christus sich selbst neu? Das schafft er nur in uns und durch uns! Die Christengemeinschaft nennt sich selbst eine Bewegung für

---

3   Offb 21,5.

religiöse Erneuerung, und dies mit Recht. Sie ist kein Standpunkt für religiöse Erneuerung, sie ist auch keine Bewegung für neue Religiosität. Die Christengemeinschaft ist vor allem eine Bewegung für Erneuerung, und diese Erneuerung erweist sich dann als religiös. In dieser Erneuerung möchte auch Christus sich selbst neu schaffen, was letztendlich besagt, dass auch das Göttliche sich entwickelt. In unserer Adventsepistel wird genau das unzweideutig ausgesprochen. Da hören wir, wie das Weltenwort, der Logos zu uns sagt: »Werde«. Und dann wird gesagt, dass sich in diesem Werden des Menschen nichts weniger als Gottes Werden vollzieht. Ich bin der Meinung, dass wir nicht aufhören sollen, dieses ketzerische Wort zutiefst zu schätzen. In gewissem Sinne soll die Christengemeinschaft sich darüber freuen, dass sie häretisch ist und versuchen, es auch so lange wie möglich zu bleiben. Denn nur, indem wir das Göttliche als das Unvollendete betrachten, als eine Zukunftskraft, die auf uns Menschen wartet, werden wir dafür Sorge tragen können, dass Christus sich in uns, durch uns und an uns erneuern kann.[4] Das wäre wahre Christengemeinschaft.

Auch das wurde uns 1922 ans Herz gelegt. Man kann sagen, dass vor zweitausend Jahren Christus

---

[4] »Ich bin bei euch alle Tage bis an der Welt Ende.« Mt 28,20.

sich mit jedem Menschen-Ich verbunden hat. Dieses wahre Menschenwesen, unser ewiges Ich, worin Christus selbst lebt, wird, so sagt Rudolf Steiner bei der Gründung, in jeder Menschenweihehandlung hereingerufen.[5] Letztendlich ist es deswegen nur dort, in unserem höheren Ich, dass wir einen Halt finden können. Nach diesem Halt sehnen wir uns eigentlich alle. Denn wir leben in einer Welt, die immer tumultuarischer wird. Immer mehr wird es eine Herausforderung, die innere Ruhe zu behalten. Man könnte sagen, dass jedes Ich in gewissem Sinne eine Weltenmitte ist. Das sich erneuernde Weltenwort lebt im Ich. Das heißt, dass der Logos, das Weltenwort, auch die Mitte der Welt ist. Es ist dort, in dieser Mitte, dass wir uns wahrhaft getragen fühlen können.

1922, einige Monate vor der Gründung der Christengemeinschaft, wurde in Wien der große West-Ost-Kongress in der Anthroposophischen Gesellschaft organisiert. In diesem Kongress lebte die Frage nach der geopolitischen Mitte der Welt. Die Mitte gibt es tatsächlich nicht nur in uns, es gibt sie auch in der Welt, oder sie sollte es zumindest geben, wo Ost und West in ihren jeweiligen Einseitigkeiten ausgeglichen werden.

---

5 Rudolf Steiner, GA 344: *Vorträge und Kurse über christlich-religiöses Wirken III*, 12. Vortrag.

Man könnte sagen, dass jede Mitte immer eine Mitte innerhalb von Extremen ist. Der englische Historiker Eric Hobsbawm hat das 20. Jahrhundert »*the age of extremes*« genannt, das Zeitalter der Extreme. Es ist inzwischen deutlich, dass das 21. Jahrhundert sich nicht weniger extrem auslebt als das 20. Jahrhundert, auch was die Angelegenheit von Ost und West betrifft. Die Mitte scheint zu verdampfen.

Vor zweitausend Jahren ertönte das Wort: »Das Reich Gottes ist nahe.« Wir gehen wohl nicht fehl, wenn wir sagen, dass heute, im 21. Jahrhundert, das Reich des Teufels nahe ist, vielleicht sogar so nah wie nie zuvor. Aber auch das muss sein. Christus erneuert sich, indem er durch die Individualität hindurchgeht. Indem er das tut, wird das Weltenwort nicht nur individuell. Es ist unvermeidlich, dass der Logos sich in seinem Gang durch die Menschheit auch verdünnt. Das Dünnerwerden des Weltenwortes, womit Geistverweigerung, Chaos und Extreme verbunden sind, dasjenige also, womit unsere Kultur so ungeheuer stark zu kämpfen hat, dieses Nahesein des Teufelsreichs, all dies muss aber nicht nur etwas Negatives sein. Aus der Homöopathie wissen wir, dass eine Verdünnung auch eine Potenzierung ist. Durch jedes individuelle Ich geht Christus hindurch. Das ist sein Weltenwille. Jedes Ich wird in diesem Prozess an die Grenzen seiner Möglichkeiten gebracht. Gerade in diesem höchst riskanten Geschehen, wo der Geist fast unerträglich dünn wird, erreicht das Weltenwort aber auch etwas, was es ohne diesen Vorgang nie hätte erreichen können. Etwas ganz Neues schimmert durch.

In dem Dünnerwerden des Weltenwortes, das wir alle irgendwie miterleben, bewusst oder unbewusst, wird das Weltenwort auch stärker: Es wird unsichtbarer, aber dafür umso wirksamer.

In einem Vortrag über das Weltenwort sagt Rudolf Steiner, dass der Logos, das Weltenwort, nicht irgendeine Silbenzusammensetzung ist, sondern dasjenige, was aus unzähligen und unzähligen Wesen zusammentönt.[6] Zu diesen unzähligen und unzähligen Wesen gehören auch wir. In uns möchte das Weltenwort tönen, indem es sich selbst verdünnt und dadurch erneuert. In dem Sinne ist die Individualisierung das Nadelöhr aller Entwicklung. Das ist der Grund, weswegen die Christengemeinschaft überhaupt erstehen sollte. Die Weihehandlung ist uns gegeben worden, damit wir wahrlich bei uns selbst sein können. Denn erst indem wir bei uns selbst ankommen, werden wir auch ankommen bei dem

---

6 Rudolf Steiner, GA 230: *Der Mensch als Zusammenklang des schaffenden, bildenden und gestaltenden Weltenwortes*, 9. Vortrag.

Göttlichen, das in uns wohnt. Das ist es, was Rudolf Steiner meinte, als er sagte, dass in jeder Menschenweihehandlung das wahre, höhere Ich der Anwesenden hereingerufen wird. Das ist es, was die große Idee, die Säule, das lebendige Wesen der Menschenweihehandlung für uns ermöglicht.

Wir leben in einer Welt, in der es uns recht schwer gemacht wird, wirklich bei uns selbst zu sein. Ständig werden wir vom Wesentlichen abgelenkt. Das ist nicht nur Kulturkritik. Es hat auch damit zu tun, dass wir in gewissem Sinne immer von uns selbst getrennt sind, und zwar konstitutiv. Wir verfügen über ein zeitliches und ein ewiges Wesen, und das Zeitliche ist grundsätzlich vom Ewigen getrennt. Mit dieser Trennung ist ein wichtiges Geheimnis unserer Zeit verbunden, das auch für das Mitvollziehen der Weihehandlung bedeutsam ist. Dieses Geheimnis hat mit dem genauen Ort der Schwelle zur geistigen Welt zu tun. Diese Schwelle befindet sich nämlich nicht am Mond, oder sonst irgendwo ganz weit entfernt, sondern geht quer durch uns hindurch. Die Schwelle ist dasjenige, was uns trennt von uns selbst, und die Weihehandlung ist uns gegeben worden, damit wir diese Trennung von uns selbst gut überstehen und sogar überwinden können. Wenn wir das Ewige in uns selbst gefunden haben, dann finden wir auch den Logos in uns. Dann haben wir die

Weltenmitte in uns verwirklicht, die Mitte, die in dieser Welt traurigerweise kaum zu finden ist heute.

Man kann sagen, dass vor hundert Jahren das Ost-West-Problem nicht gelöst worden ist, dass es 1989 nicht gelöst worden ist, und dass es sicherlich nicht dabei ist, heute gelöst zu werden. Die Weltenmitte scheint überall bedroht zu werden. Noch vor zwei Jahren, 2020, haben wir erleben müssen, wie in einer Epidemiebekämpfung das Kollektiv auf einmal viel wichtiger als das Individuelle befunden wurde. Wer auf das Individuum rechnen wollte, wer die eigene Individualität gelten lassen mochte, wurde gesellschaftlich als fragwürdig angesehen. Der Kampf gegen die Individualität, das heißt: der Kollektivismus, ist aber immer auch ein Kampf gegen Christus. Wenn wir die Weltenmitte nicht äußerlich politisch schaffen, dann sollen wir sie zumindest doch innerlich schaffen. Die Menschenweihehandlung wird uns dabei eine verlässliche Stütze sein. Wenn wir uns verbinden mit den Kräften, die in ihr freigesetzt werden, dann gibt es trotz aller Wirrnisse einen Weg vorwärts.

Seit es die Christengemeinschaft gibt, ist es nie ruhig gewesen auf Erden. In den letzten zwanzig Jahren, einem Fünftel der Geschichte der Christengemeinschaft, sind wir eigentlich nur von Krise zu Krise gegangen. 2001 gab es die Anschläge in New York und 2003 die amerikanische Invasion im Irak; 2008 gab es den weltweiten finanziellen Kollaps; 2016 gab es die Flüchtlingskrise; 2020 gab es eine Epidemie und die globale Überreaktion darauf. Jetzt, 2022, gibt es wieder Krieg in Europa. Wir können ohne Weiteres davon ausgehen, dass auch die nächsten zwanzig Jahre nicht ruhiger sein werden. Die Säule der Christengemeinschaft aber, diese Säule des Weltenwortes, sie ist da, sie begleitet uns, und sie bewegt sich mit uns. In ihr finden wir die Ruhe, in ihr finden wir eine Mitte in *the age of extremes*, in ihr finden wir den Frieden. In diesem Frieden finden wir Christus, und findet er uns. Wenn wir es schaffen, dass die Christengemeinschaft wirklich Form innerhalb von Bewegung bleibt, wenn wir es hinbekommen, dass wir wie Bienen sind, die frohen Mutes in die Welt fliegen, weil sie trotz aller Hässlichkeit, Tragik und Grausamkeit *auch* schön, sanft und gut ist, wenn es uns gelingt, die Christengemeinschaft so in die Welt zu tragen, dass sie ein Gefäß der tätigen Liebe ist, in dem manche Worte vielleicht sogar duften statt stinken, dann haben wir die allerbeste Hoffnung, dass sie auch in den nächsten hundert Jahren richtig in die Welt hineingestellt wird. In dieser Gesinnung, denke ich, können wir diese unsere Tagung heiter und hoffnungsfroh anfangen.

Mathijs van Alstein

The Promise
of the Unfinished

Dear friends!

Exactly one hundred years ago the spoken word was
activated like never before. Because it was in this year,
more precisely in October 1922, that the BBC was founded. When I was a kid in the eighties, I used to enjoy
listening to local programs on the radio in the evening.
Sometimes the announcer would say – and I remember
this vividly – »Dear folks, we're back on the airwaves,
we're back in the ether!« Looking back, it certain-
ly couldn't have been a coincidence that the BBC and
The Christian Community were founded in exactly the
same year, in more or less the same weeks even. We can
indeed say: a hundred years ago the etheric world opened up in such a way that presenters could speak into
a microphone and reach hundreds of thousands, even
millions of households. At the same time, the etheric
world opened up in such a way that the new liturgical
word could resound in it. Both events, the technical and
the liturgic, seem to belong together. They are two sides

of the same coin. In the hundred years we look back upon today, the media has undergone a rapid development. We are all caught up in the consequences of this development, and not all of them are pleasant. In the 1880's, a German philosopher with a very clear vision about things to come said something astonishing. That philosopher's name was Friedrich Nietzsche. In 1882 he wrote: »Another hundred years of newspapers – and all words will stink.«[1]

More than a century later we have to admit there was some truth to his assertion. We haven't just undergone an inflation in the financial sphere, where one dollar in 1922 was worth seventeen dollar in today's money. Words have also devalued over time. Not all words stink today; nevertheless, a pure word has become increasingly rare. Each word seems to drown in the next. In this world, with its staggering abundance of written and spoken words, The Christian Community tries to thrive. For a hundred years now we have been gathering regularly to hear the spoken word in the etheric world, calm and peaceful and utterly untechnological.

What is the nature of this liturgical word? The word of the act of consecration of man, which is very

---

[1] Friedrich Nietzsche, *Nachgelassene Fragmente.* Sommer-Herbst 1882.

dear to us all, is spoken out of a being. This being is called the word of the world, the *Logos*. Out of the great speaking of the universe, a distillation of this word of the world dwells on the lips of the celebrating priest. Thus the act of consecration of man becomes a being within a being, a word within a word: just like the *Logos* itself it exists in the realm of independent beings. Have we recognized this entity yet? Have we truly encountered it?

If we wish to gain a deeper understanding of the act of consecration, we first have to acknowledge that this ritual predates 1922, that it existed long before The Christian Community was founded. This may seem like a strange statement. How can something exist before it exists? How are we to understand this? Well, we can say that the act of consecration of man is a supersensible pillar that moves through the centuries, sometimes visible, sometimes unvisible. It is always here, waiting to materialize. In fact, this pillar is even older than Christ's deed on Golgotha. For the act of consecration has been around since human beings have been graciously accompanied by their gods, that is since the beginning of time. This pillar is as old as the oldest temple. If we consider the human body to be a temple, like Saint Paul does, it actually is as old as the human body. This pillar of the act of consecration of man –

which has been moving for millennia, guiding humanity in all its incantations – is conscious. It is aware of itself in all its metamorphoses, from the rituals in the ancient mysteries to the catholic mass to our own act of celebration today. To whom does this consciousness belong? It belongs to the gods themselves. One hierarchy of these venerable entities is called the spirits of form, the *Exousiai*. The Old Testament says they include the Elohim, or creators of the world. These beings are very important if we want to do justice to the act of consecration as a conscious reality. Who are these spirits of form? What exactly do they create? The Greek word for form is *eidos*, which means idea. According to both Plato and Aristotle, ideas are substances more important and more real than the ones in the material world. Plato considers them to be other-worldly, Aristotle is of the opinion they belong to our world, but both thinkers agreed that ideas are non-human in origin and form the foundation of the world. Only when we take seriously the fact that the act of consecration of man is a conscious being, an idea, a form that moves more invisibly than visibly through time, can we start to understand why it is written that Christ's passion, his revelation, and his resurrection all think in us. During the act of consecration, we think and feel; yet we are also thought and felt by spiritual beings! These spirits of form, who create ideas in the cosmos, who lift us humans up into their thoughts and feelings, also operate within another hierarchy. This hierarchy is called the *Dynameis*, the spirits of movement. They are also very important, for The Christian Community is not only a matter of form, which is obvious in its liturgy, it is also primarily a movement. We don't call ourselves a »movement for religious renewal« for no reason. If we want to understand The Christian Community correctly, we must say: it is form within movement, just as the spirits of form operate within spirits of movement. The movement embraces the form. That's how it is with the hierarchies up above and that's how it should be with us down below. The Christian Community aspires to be form in movement.

It is quite remarkable that in the same week as the foundation of The Christian Community, after all the newly ordained men and women had left Dornach, Rudolf Steiner gave another lecture about ceremonial acts. This lecture was not for the priests-to-be of course, but for the anthroposophists who had not participated in the foundation of The Christian Community and who were therefore not connected to this religious renewal. The last lecture at the foundation was given on September 22, 1922. On September 24, 1922, not more than forty-eight hours after the ancient substance of the consecration of man had been reshaped, Rudolf Steiner was able to speak soberly about the dangers associated with liturgical forms – seemingly unimpressed by the great event that had just occurred. This talk cannot be found in the lecture cycles about The Christian Community and is therefore easy to overlook. But what was said in this lecture is very important, and I think we should consider its content as an essential part of our founding. In this lecture, Rudolf Steiner talks about the Egyptian mysteries and how the mummy was used in them.[2] As modernity is a metamorphosis or a kind of repetition of Egyptian culture, it should come as no surprise that the mummy, that is to say its atrophying quality, returns in modernity as well. And here Rudolf Steiner says – let me repeat, within forty-eight hours after The Christian Community was founded – that the metamorphosed mummy is the liturgy! He is talking about catholic and freemason rituals here. Nevertheless, it is very difficult not to take this statement as a warning directly addressed to us. Why was it necessary, right after the act of consecration was born anew, only two days after its reincarnation, to speak about it possibly being *dead*? It goes without saying that the days and weeks that pre-

---

2 Rudolf Steiner, GA 216: *Die Grundimpulse des weltgeschichtlichen Werdens der Menschheit*, 5th lecture.

ceded this lecture were anything but barren. But that shouldn't lull us to sleep! Religious ceremonies can freeze and become a dead vessel, in which all kinds of spirits and ghosts do their mischief. This looming possibility apparently occupied Rudolf Steiner right after the foundation of The Christian Community. The logical question is: How does a ritual die? How does it lose its life? How does it become a mummy of itself?

Rituals die when their forms become stronger than the life they are supposed to express, when they are no longer capable of being form in motion, like they should be, but instead become some kind of activity within given and unquestioned forms, and nothing more. Dear friends, this is no small admission! In my opinion, we should take Rudolf Steiner's lecture of September 24th as a caution that a hundred years after the foundation of The Christian Community we cannot turn our movement for religious renewal into some kind of etheric bunker, where we huddle together to defend ourselves against an evil world. Because if we do this, if we become nothing but movement within form, if we have forms that we love, but love in such a way that we are active only in and through them, well, then we'll end up doing an injustice to our rituals. Because then we will have placed form above movement. This is not how the hierarchies above operate, and I think we would be ill-advised to arrange the relationships between form and movement differently on earth than in the heavens.

How then, do we manage to be form in motion, rather than motion in form? The image I have in mind here is very simple, I must admit, but nevertheless adequate. What we should aim to accomplish, I think, is an inner activity, a mobility of mind and spirit, which makes it possible for us to enter these religious forms, live with them, even feeling comfortable in them, but not without us being able *to come out* of them, like bees going into a beehive to do their business before flying into the great wide open again. If we can manage to shape our religiosity in such a way that it can operate both within and outside of ceremonial forms, it will become abundantly clear that the forms, these religious ideas, are serving life and not the other way around. And this is how it should be. The New Testament calls the church the *ekklesia*. Ekklesia comes from ek-kalein, which means »to call out«. We as members of the church are the ones who are called *out*, not the ones who are called *in*! We shouldn't try to protect ourselves from an outside world by seeking some sort of shelter in church. Instead we should joyfully integrate with reality as a whole, connect ourselves deeply with it, not flee it. Only then can the ongoing foundation of The Christian Community truly be realized.

A colleague of mine, Tom Tritschel, said something in this regard that I thought was wonderful. I'm sure he won't mind that I quote him here today. Christ says he makes all things new.[3] This, Tom said during a synod in Berlin, we should recognize as an all-encompassing statement. When Christ makes all things new, he also makes *himself* new. I had never really thought of that before, but it immediately struck a chord with me. How could it be otherwise? Everything means everything, right? But how does Christ make himself new? That, of course, is the next question. And the answer, I think, has to be this: If Christ renews himself, as he says he does, he can only do so in and through us. You can spend a lifetime thinking about this. The Christian Community calls itself a movement for religious renewal, and rightly so. We are not a monument to religious renewal, nor are we a movement for new religiosity. The Christian Community is first and foremost a movement for renewal, and this renewal then proves itself to be religious. In this process of renewal, Christ also recreates himself; ultimately, the divine is evolving, just as we are. It is one of the greater gifts of our rituals that exactly this is expressed in our Advent epistle. Here we hear how the word of the world, the *Logos*, gives us the

---

3 Rev. 21, 5.

grandest of all assignments: »Become«. And then it is said that in this becoming of man, God's becoming is being completed. I firmly believe we should not cease to appreciate this heretical utterance, for that is precisely what this is. The Christian Community should rejoice in the fact that she is unorthodox. For only by seeing the divine as unfinished, as incomplete, as a future force waiting for us, will we be able to ensure that Christ can continue to renew himself in us, through us, and unto us. Only then can we be true to to our own foundation and the promise it entailed.[4]

This close connection between human and divine becoming gets to the heart of what esoteric Christianity reveals. One can say that two thousand years ago Christ united his destiny with that of man. This unification did not only occur in Jesus. Christ became present in every single individual, welcoming into his sphere every creature that calls itself an I. Christ himself lives in this eternal I, which is in every single individual and is evoked, according to Rudolf Steiner, during every act of consecration of man.[5] In the end it is only here, in our higher self, that we can find a hold in life, something I think we all deeply long for. We live in a world

4 »I am with you always, to the end of age.« Matth. 28:20.

5 Rudolf Steiner, GA 344 *Vorträge und Kurse über christlich-religiöses Wirken III*, 12th lecture.

that is becoming more tumultuous by the day. It has become quite a challenge to keep calm. One could say that every human I is the center of a world. The word of the world lives in this I. That is where it renews itself. This means that the *logos*, the divine word that speaks in and through every living being, is also the center of the world. It is here, in this center, that we can find the steadfastness we all crave for.

In 1922, a few months before the foundation of The Christian Community, a great East-West Congress was organized by the Anthroposophical Society in Vienna. During this congress participants extensively discussed the geopolitical center of the world, what it is and what it could do. The center of the world should not only exist within us. It could also exist in the world, where East and West sould be balanced by a third in the middle. One could say that every center is always surrounded by extremes. In fact, the English historian Eric Hobsbawm called the 20th century »the age of extremes«. It is clear by now that the 21st century is no less extreme than the 20th century, including, as we currently are witnessing, the collision between East and West. The middle seems to be evaporating.

Two thousand years ago the words rang out, »The kingdom of God is at hand«. We are probably not wrong in saying that today, in the 21st century, the devil's kingdom is at hand, perhaps like never before. But this, too, must be. Christ renews himself by passing through each individuality. By doing this, the word of the world becomes not only individual. It is inevitable that the *Logos* also dilutes in its passing through humanity. This thinning out of the cosmic word brings along a denial of the spirit, chaos and all sorts of extremes. But these troubles that our world has to struggle with so tremendously today do not need to be only negative. Homeopathy teaches us that a dilution is also a potentiation. Christ passes through every individual ego. This is his celestial will. Each human being is brought to the limits of its potential in this process. This highly risky endeavour, which renders the spirit almost unbearably thin, also allows the world-word to achieve something it could never attain otherwise. Something completely new shimmers through. In the thinning out of the *Logos* – something we all consciously or unconsciously experience – the divine word also becomes more potent. It becomes more invisible, but all the more effective because of it.

In a lecture on the *Logos*, Rudolf Steiner says that the cosmic word is not just a composition of mere syllables, but something that sounds together from an innumerable and countless array of beings.[6] We humans also belong amongst these innumerable and countless beings. We are members of the great choir of reality. In the human being the world-word can resonate by diluting itself and thereby renewing itself. In this sense, individualization is like going through the eye of the needle in terms of development. This is the reason why The Christian Community had to come into existence in the first place. The act of consecration of man has been given to us as a means of aligning with ourselves. For only by arriving at ourselves will we able to arrive at the divine that dwells within us. This is what Rudolf Steiner meant when he said that every act of consecration evokes the truer, higher self of those present. This is what the great idea, the pillar, the living essence of the act of consecration, makes possible for us.

We live in a world where it has become increasingly difficult to really be with ourselves. We are constantly being distracted from the essential. This is not just cheap cultural criticism. It also has to do with the profound spiritual fact that we are *always* separated from ourselves, and constitutionally so. We have a temporal and an eternal being. What gets born at the beginning

---

6 Rudolf Steiner, GA 230: *Der Mensch als Zusammenklang des schaffenden, bildenden und gestaltenden Weltenwortes*, 9th lecture.

of life and what dies at the end of it is not our eternal self. This eternal self remains hovering above us, so to speak. It is both unborn and immortal. This is our true being. The temporal self is fundamentally separate from this eternal one; if it would be any otherwise, we would instantly remember our life before we were born as well as our previous incarnations. This, of course, is not the case. Human memory only becomes active in the second or third year of our lives. This separation from what is unborn and immortal is deeply connected with an important mystery of our time. Our comprehension of the act of consecration is also linked to this mystery. It pertains to the exact location of the threshold to the spiritual world. This threshold is not to be found on the moon or somewhere else far away. It runs straight through us. This thinly veiled demarcation is what separates us from ourselves, and the act of consecration was given to us so that we could learn to overcome this separation. When we find the eternal in ourselves, we also find the *Logos*. Here we will find the center that is so under pressure in our world.

The East-West problem wasn't solved a hundred years ago. It wasn't solved in 1989 either, and clearly won't be solved any time soon. The middleground seems to be under siege wherever you look. Only two years ago, in 2020, we witnessed how the collective was given preference over the individual in the context of an epidemic. Many who favored the individual, who wanted to assess the situation from their own individuality, were considered dissidents. But prohibitions of individuality and enforced collectivism are also fights against the Christ-being. This was one of the main lessons of the 20th century. If we are unable to create the middle of the world externally, that is to say politically, we can at least try to establish it inwardly. Here the act of consecration of man can be a reliable haven. If we truly relate to the forces released in this ritual, we might just find a way forward amidst all the confusion.

It has not been quiet on earth since The Christian Community was founded. The violence, lies and catastrophes that struck humanity in the years between 1922 and 2022 are without any historical precedent. In the last twenty years – one fifth of the history of The Christian Community – we have basically been shuffling from one crisis to the next. In 2001 we witnessed the attacks in New York and in 2003 the American invasion of Iraq; in 2008 we had the great financial collapse; a refugee crisis began in 2016; in 2020 there was an epidemic and the global overreaction to it; in 2022 Europe is at war again. It is only fair to assume that the next twenty years will not be any calmer. But the pillar of The Christian Community, this supernatural column of the gods uniting with their creation, is here to stay. It moves along with us through all of our earthly troubles and strife. In it we can find tranquility and a calm eye in the storm of extremes. In it we can find our peace. In this peace we find Christ, as he finds us. If we do our very best to make sure The Christian Community remains form within movement, as it is intended, if we can fly into the world like bees, recognizing that this world is *also* beautiful, gentle and good, despite all its ugliness, tragedy and cruelty, if we succeed in carrying The Christian Community into the world like this, in such a way that it can become a place of active love, where some words actually may even smell good, well, then we have the very best hope that our movement will find its proper place in the next hundred years. In this spirit, I think, we can begin this conference of ours cheerfully and with confidence indeed.

Mathijs van Alstein wurde 1976 in Belgien geboren. Nach dem Besuch der Waldorfschule studierte er Philosophie an den Universitäten Antwerpen, Brüssel und Leuven und promovierte über das Thema »Hören auf das Sein: Heideggers Lehre vom Logos«. 2006 kam er an das Hamburger Priesterseminar. Im Jahr 2010 empfing er die Priesterweihe und wurde nach Zeist, Holland, entsandt. Im Verlag Urachhaus erschien im Herbst 2022: *Versuche in der Leere. Von der Leidenschaft zur Erkenntnis.* Mathijs van Alstein ist verheiratet und hat zwei Kinder.

Mathijs van Alstein was born in Belgium in 1976. After attending the Steiner School he studied philosophy at the Universities of Antwerp, Brussels and Leuven and wrote his doctoral thesis entitled »Hören auf das Sein: Heideggers Lehre vom Logos«. In 2006 he started his education at the priest seminary in Hamburg. He received his ordination in 2010 and was dispatched to Zeist, Netherlands. In fall 2022 Urachhaus published his first book »Versuche in der Leere. Von der Leidenschaft zur Erkenntnis«. Mathijs van Alstein is married and has two children.

Weiterführendes

Wenn dieser Band Ihr Interesse geweckt hat, können Sie die Reihe der LOGOS-edition weiter verfolgen, Informationen über die Christengemeinschaft online finden, unsere Zeitschriften lesen oder die Beiträge der Tagung als Podcast anhören.

Die LOGOS-edition im Verlag Urachhaus

Als Nr. 2 der Reihe wird in Kürze folgende Vortragsnachschrift über den Buchhandel erhältlich sein:
Dr. Georg Soldner, *Der Heilungsimpuls im Lukas-Evangelium.*

Sammelbestellungen können direkt über den Verlag erfolgen: vertrieb@urachhaus.com; Tel.: (+49) 0711 28532-32

Folgende Autorinnen und Autoren haben zugesagt, ihre Vortragsnachschriften für den Druck in der LOGOS-edition zu bearbeiten: Lisa Devine, Susanne Gödecke, Michaela Glöckler, Gisela Thriemer, Michael Debus, Volker Harlan, Claudio Holland, Christward Kröner, Stephan Meyer, Jarosław Rolka, Oliver Steinrueck, Johannes Stüttgen, João Torunsky, Tom Tritschel. Weitere sind angefragt.

Die Tagung

Viele Informationen zur Tagung *LOGOS – Consecrating Humanity* finden Sie auch weiterhin auf der Tagungs-Website: https://cg-2022. org/wp/

Die Podcasts vor und nach der Tagung

Hören Sie auch in die spannende Podcastreihe zur Tagung und zur Zukunft der Christengemeinschaft hinein. Die Logos Podcast Initiative hat am 22. Februar 2021 ihren ersten Podcast online gestellt. Es sind als Vorbereitung der Tagung insgesamt 20 Podcasts von ungefähr 22 Minuten veröffentlicht worden, in deutscher und englischer Sprache.

Logos-Podcast: https://soundcloud.com/user-895241549

Die Christengemeinschaft – Bewegung für religiöse Erneuerung

Weitere allgemeine Informationen über die Christengemeinschaft finden Sie auf diesen Websites:

https://christengemeinschaft.de/

https://christengemeinschaft-international.org/

Zeitschriften

Es gibt Zeitschriften der Christengemeinschaft in unterschiedlichen Sprachen, z.B.:

»Die Christengemeinschaft – Zeitschrift zur religiösen Erneuerung«:
https://www.urachhaus.de/Zeitschriften/Die-Christengemein-schaft.html

»Perspectives«, England

http://thechristiancommunity.co.uk/PVS-test/portfolio-items/perspectives-2005/

»In beweging«, Niederlande
https://christengemeenschap.nl/in-beweging/

Paulus Fonds für religiöses Schrifttum

Wir danken dem Paulus Fonds der internationalen Christengemeinschaft für die finanzielle Förderung der LOGOS-edition. Zuwendungen sind dort herzlich willkommen:

Die Christengemeinschaft in Deutschland
Bankverbindung:
IBAN: DE16 8502 0500 0003 6204 00
BIC: BFSWDE33DRE

Further Information

If this book has piqued your interest, you can continue to follow the LOGOS-edtion series, find information about the Christian Community online, read our magazines, or listen to the conference contributions as a podcast.

The LOGOS-edition in the publishing house Urachhaus
The following lecture transcript will be available through bookstores in December as vol. 2:
Dr. Georg Soldner, *The Healing Impulse in the Gospel of Luke.*

Collective orders can be made directly through the publisher: vertrieb@urachhaus.com; Tel.: (+49) 0711 28532-32

The following authors have agreed to edit their lecture transcripts for printing in the LOGOS-edition: Lisa Devine, Susanne Gödecke, Michaela Glöckler, Gisela Thriemer, Michael Debus, Volker Harlan, Claudio Holland, Christward Kröner, Stephan Meyer, Jarosław Rolka, Oliver Steinrueck, Johannes Stüttgen, João Torunsky, Tom Tritschel. Others are requested.

The conference
You will continue to find a lot of information about the LOGOS – Consecrating Humanity conference on the conference website: https://cg-2022.org/wp/.

Podcasts – before and after the conference

You can also listen to the exciting podcast series about the conference and the future of the Christian Community. The Logos Podcast Initiative launched its first podcast online on February 22, 2021. A total of 20 podcasts of about 22 minutes have been published in preparation for the conference, in German and English.

Logos podcast: https://soundcloud.com/user-895241549

The Christian Community – Movement for religious Renewal

You can find more general information about The Christian Community on these websites:

https://christengemeinschaft.de/

https://christengemeinschaft-international.org/

https://www.thechristiancommunity.org/

https://www.thechristiancommunity.net/

http://www.thechristiancommunity.co.uk/

Magazines

The Christian Community magazines are available in different languages, e.g.:

»The Christian Community« – Journal for Religious Renewal (in German)

https://www.urachhaus.de/Zeitschriften/Die-Christengemeinschaft.html

»Perspectives« – from the Christian Community in England
http://thechristiancommunity.co.uk/PVS-test/portfolio-items/
perspectives-2005/

»In beweging« – from the Christian Community in the Netherlands
https://christengemeenschap.nl/in-beweging/

Paulus Fund for Religious Literature

We would like to thank the Paulus Fund of the international
Christian Community for the financial support of the LOGOS-
edition. Financial contributions to the fund are welcome any time.

Bank details:
Die Christengemeinschaft in Deutschland
IBAN: DE16 8502 0500 0003 6204 00
BIC: BFSWDE33DRE

FSC
www.fsc.org

MIX

Papier | Fördert
gute Waldnutzung

FSC® C083411

Druck:
CPI Druckdienstleistungen GmbH
im Auftrag der
Zeitfracht GmbH
Ein Unternehmen der Zeitfracht - Gruppe
Ferdinand-Jühlke-Str. 7
99095 Erfurt